ABUNDANT TRUTH INTERNATIONAL MINISTRIES

Ministry Guides Series

The Believer's Guide to the Pastoral Ministry

A Comprehensive Study of the Pastoral Ministry in the Church

Roderick Levi Evans

The Believer's Guide to the Pastoral Ministry
A Comprehensive Study of the Pastoral Ministry in the Church

All Rights Reserved ©2024 by Roderick L. Evans

No part of this book may be reproduced or transmitted in any form or by any means, graphic, electronic, or mechanical, including photocopying, recording, taping, or by any information storage or retrieval system, without the permission in writing from the publisher.

Front & Back Cover Designs by Abundant Truth Publishing

Abundant Truth Publishing
an imprint of Abundant Truth International Ministries

For information address:
Abundant Truth International
P.O. Box 126
Camden, NC 27921

Unless otherwise indicated, all of the scripture quotations are taken from the *Authorized King James Version* of the Bible. Scripture quotations marked with NIV are taken from the *New International Version* of the Bible. Scripture quotations marked with NASV are taken from the *New American Standard Version* of the Bible. Scripture quotations marked with Amplified are taken from the *Amplified Bible*.

ISBN: 978-1-60141-636-0

Printed in the United States of America

Contents

Introduction

Book 1 – The Yoking of the Pastor	**1**
Introduction	3
Chapter 1- Yoking of the Pastor	**7**
Submission	10
Hardships	11
Chapter 2 - Love of the Pastor	**15**
The Love of the Church	18
The Impartation of the Word	19
The Personal Zeal	21
Chapter 3 - Building of the Pastor	**23**
Pastoral Care	26
Pastoral Wisdom	27
Pastoral Authority	28
Pastoral Burden	29
Chapter 4 - The Pastor's Character	**33**
Blameless	34
Husband of One Wife	35

Contents (cont.)

Vigilant	36
Sober	37
Good Behavior	38
Given to Hospitality	39
Apt to Teach	39
Not given to wine	40
Not a striker, Not a brawler	41
Not Greedy for Money or Covetous	42
Patient	42
Rules own house well	43

Book 2 – I Will Give You Pastors — 45
Introduction — 47

Chapter 1 – What is a Pastor? — 51
The Facts of Pastoral Ministry — 55
The Function of Pastoral Ministry — 57
The Focal Point of Pastoral Ministry — 61

Chapter 2 – The Call of a Pastor — 63
Perceiving the Pastoral Call — 66

Contents (cont.)

Preparing for the Pastoral Call   70
Performing the Pastoral Call   75

Chapter 3 – The Office of the Pastor   **81**
Nine Functions of the Pastoral Office   83
The Focus of Pastoral Ministry   94

Chapter 4 – The Roles of Pastors   **97**
Pastors as Fathers   100
Pastors as Watchmen   112

Chapter 5 – False Pastors   **119**
Characteristics of False Ministers   123
Characteristics of False Pastors   127

Book 3 – Keys to Pastoral Ministry and Recovery   **133**
Introduction   135

Chapter 1 - Prologue: The Lysterian Legacy   **139**
Deification of Leaders   143
Reluctancy of Leaders   144

Contents (cont.)

Chapter 2 - The David Dilemma	**147**
Emotional Influences	153
Social Influences	155
Chapter 3 – The Recovery of Manasseh	**157**
Humility	162
Overcome Fear	163
Ask	164
Listen/follow Through	165
Accountability	166
Chapter 4 – Creating an Atmosphere	**167**
Messages of Love	171
Motivate the leaders	172
Mobilize the Masses	172
Book 4 – The Perfecting of the Pastoral Person	**175**
Introduction	177
Prologue: Understanding Anointings	**185**
Anointings in the Old Testament	186
Anointings in the New Testament	190

Contents (cont.)

Office versus Anointing — 196

Chapter 1- Pastoral People are Undershepherds — **201**
Spiritual Providers — 203
Spiritual Imparters — 204
Spiritual Discipline — 205
Spiritual Protectors — 206

Chapter 2 - Pastoral People are Menservansts & Maidservants — **209**
A Servant's Care — 211
A Servant's Submission — 212

Chapter 3 - Character Traits of Pastoral People — **215**
Love of the Body of Christ — 217
Faithful in the Body of Christ — 218
Building of the Body of Christ — 219

Chapter 4 – Realizing the Pastoral Anointing — **221**
Understanding Scriptures — 223

Contents (cont.)

Understanding Impartation	224
Understanding Prayer	225
Understanding Authority	226
Understanding Gifts	228
Chapter 5 – Flowing in the Pastoral Anointing	**231**
Consistent in Study	233
Consistent in Prayer	234
Consistent in Submission	235
Bibliography	**237**

Introduction

Ministry and service are gifts from God. The ministries are multifaceted and sometimes complex. The Ministry Guides Series is designed to offer information that will strengthen, enlighten, and encourage those involved in Christian ministry.

In this publication

In this book, we will bring clarity to the roles of pastors, the functionality of pastoral ministry, and the expressions of the pastoral gift. This study is comprised of 3 distinct works on the pastoral office and gift:

1) The Yoking of the Pastor: The Preparation of the Pastor for Ministry and Service
2) I Will Give You Pastors: Examining the Pastoral Office in the New Testament Church
3) Keys to Pastoral Ministry and Recovery: Help for Wounded Healer
4) The Perfecting of the Pastoral Person: The Preparation of the Pastoral Person for Ministry and Service

It is our prayer that a greater understanding and appreciation for the prophetic gift and ministry will be achieved.

THE BELIEVER'S GUIDE TO THE PASTORL MINISTRY — A Comprehensive Study of the Pastoral Ministry in the Church

-Book 1-

The Yoking of the Pastor:

The Preparation of the Pastor and Prophetic Minister for Ministry and Service

The training of a prophet is sometimes painful. God will deal with every area in his life to prepare him for service. Those called to the prophetic office should understand that preparation for ministry is in character, not solely in the development of spiritual gifts. In this book, we will discuss how God builds the prophet and prophetic minister for ministry.

THE BELIEVER'S GUIDE TO THE PASTORL MINISTRY — A Comprehensive Study of the Pastoral Ministry in the Church

Introduction

Ministry and service in the kingdom of God is a privilege. God calls every member of the Body of Christ to serve for the benefit and welfare of the Body of Christ. However, we must remember that there are personal preparations that God requires for service.

The Potter's Wheel Study Series is designed to help believers recognize and apply the personal preparation that God implements for those called to minister and to serve. It is our prayer that the minister and the laymen will respond to God's personal preparations for ministry and service.

THE BELIEVER'S GUIDE TO THE PASTORL MINISTRY A Comprehensive Study of the Pastoral Ministry in the Church

In this Publication

The pastor's ministry comes with authority, power, and oversight of God's people. These are only parts of the pastor's ministry. His ministry serves as a reflection of Christ's love of the Church.

Therefore, the pastor's character has to be solid. Therefore, God will take pastors through tests, trials, and temptations in order to prepare them for ministry.

The training of a pastor is oftentimes humbling. God will allow disruption in every area of his life, personally and professionally. It will prepare him for service. Those called to the pastoral office should understand that preparation for this ministry will produce spiritual maturity and strength for leading God's people.

THE BELIEVER'S GUIDE TO THE PASTORL MINISTRY A Comprehensive Study of the Pastoral Ministry in the Church

THE BELIEVER'S GUIDE TO THE PASTORL MINISTRY — A Comprehensive Study of the Pastoral Ministry in the Church

-Chapter 1-

Yoking of the Pastor:

Jeremiah's yoke

The training of a pastor is oftentimes humbling. God will allow disruption in every area of his life, personally and professionally. It will prepare him for service. Those called to the pastoral office should understand that preparation for this ministry will produce spiritual maturity and strength for leading God's people.

Jeremiah prophesied to Judah during a time of great rebellion and sin against God. To express His judgment upon Judah, God instructed Jeremiah to wear a wooden yoke to signify Judah and the others nations' impending bondage in Babylon.

> *In the beginning of the reign of Jehoiakim the son of Josiah king of Judah came this word unto Jeremiah from the LORD, saying, Thus saith the LORD to me; Make thee bonds and yokes, and put them upon thy neck. Jer 27:1-2 (KJV)*

Jeremiah's yoke represented submission to the Babylonian kingdom. When something is yoked, it is harnessed and under control. In addition, it signifies joining. This is what the Lord does to the pastor.

Submission

A pastor has to be in subjection to God while being joined to the Church. Therefore, God will allow the pastor to experience humbling situations so that he will submit to God and exercise compassion upon those whom he leads.

Without submission unto God and a love for the people, the pastor will fall into pride and arrogance. Thus, God humbles him in order to preserve him.

> *I am become a fool in glorying; ye have compelled me: for I ought to have been commended of you: for in nothing am I behind the very chiefest apostles, though I be nothing.(2 Corinthians 12:11)*

Paul spoke of his ministry, but declared he was nothing. Because of God's discipline and training, Paul walked in humility even after years of powerful ministry.

Hardships

Pastors will endure many hardships before and during ministry. God allows a continual yoking process in their lives to keep them humble and broken before him. Pastors go from one hardship to the next to keep them in subjection to God and understanding to the needs of the congregants. The suffering of the pastor mirrors that of the apostle.

> *For I think that God hath set forth us the apostles last, as it were appointed to death: for we are made a spectacle unto the world, and to angels, and to men. (I Corinthians 4:9)*

Because of the Lord's process, Paul stated that he felt as if apostles were appointed unto death. This means that the apostle will meet consistent opposition and tests. Those called to the ministry, including the pastoral office will have testimonies of great rejection, times of poverty, and sickness.

They will be the subject of gossip, debate, and slander. This ensures that the pastor will be able to speak directly and accurately into

the lives of the people.

Pastors usually experience debasing situations to produce selflessness and humility. These things will happen even after they enter into the pastorate.

There is a consistent call to selflessness laid on the pastor. His pride will consistently be broken so that Christ and the Church may shine.

We are fools for Christ's sake, but ye are wise in Christ; we are weak, but ye are strong; ye are honourable, but we are despised. (I Corinthians 4:10)

The pastor's selflessness results in a fruitful ministry and healthy Church.

Verily, verily, I say unto you, Except a corn of wheat fall into the ground and die, it abideth alone: but if it die, it bringeth forth much fruit. (John 12:24)

THE BELIEVER'S GUIDE TO THE PASTORL MINISTRY A Comprehensive Study of the Pastoral Ministry in the Church

-Chapter 2-

Love of the Pastor:

Husbands and Wives

A major part of the pastor's making is in the area of love. It is almost the same as the apostles' making. God places a deep love in the pastor for Christ and the Church.

If the pastor's love does not emulate Christ's, he will harm the flock of God. He will injure God's people.

Since pastors stand as a visible representation of Christ's love, it is important to understand that the Christ-Church relationship is marriage.

As Christ is married to the Church, so are the pastors. Husbands are to love their wives as Christ loved the Church. The pastor, then, acts as a husband to the Church.

The scriptures give guidelines for how the husband is to treat his wife (Ephesians 5:22-32; I

Peter 3:7). The same principles apply to the pastor.

The Love of the Church

Husbands must love their wives. Pastors have a deep love for the Church. They minister in the Church with the love and compassion of Christ.

Paul instructs husbands to love and lay down their lives for their wives as Christ did for the Church. The pastor's life and ministry are set-aside for the Church and the advancement of the Kingdom of God.

The scriptures tell us that Jesus became sin for us. He loved us so much that He became a curse in the eyes of man that we may live. In the above verses, Paul gives an account to the Corinthian Church of how they are suffering many things for their sakes.

Pastors are to lay down their lives for the Church, that the glory of God may be seen in the lives of the people. Jesus said.

> *Greater love hath no man than this,, that a man lay down his life for his friends. (John 15:13)*

The greatest demonstration of love by Christ was that He gave His life for us. The pastor has to be willing to do the same for the Church. He will invest time, energy, and effort into the local assembly.

The Impartation of the Word

Husbands must impart the Word to their wives. As Christ sanctified the Church by the Word, so should husbands be able to impart life to their wives by the Word.

As husbands to the Church, pastors share in the responsibility of cleansing the Church through the Word, that she may be presented unto God without spot or winkle.

The focus of the pastoral ministry is to perfect the saints in the walks with Christ. The pastor labors to ensure the success of the people until the day of Redemption.

This is accomplished through the preaching of the Word. Consider the following:

> *Now ye are clean through the word which I have spoken unto you. (John 15: 3)*

> *For I am jealous over you with godly jealousy: for I have espoused you to one husband, that I may present you as a chaste virgin to Christ. (II Corinthians 11:2)*

Jesus pronounced His disciples clean because He had preached the Word unto them. The pastor, like Christ, cleanses the Church through the Word.

The Personal Zeal

Husbands must love their wives as their own bodies. Husbands are instructed to love their wives as their own bodies. Pastors have to minister with great love.

Though they minister to the Church, they themselves are also a part of the Church. Husbands are admonished to nourish and cherish their wives as they would their own bodies.

Pastors should remember to minister to the Church as if they are ministering to themselves. The pastor and the Church will stand before the judgment seat of God.

-Chapter 3-

Building of the Pastor:

Woman in Revelation

God develops humility and love in the pastor to build them into faithful shepherds. There are general characteristics that every pastor possesses as a result of Christ's building process.

Since the pastor will reflect Christ's love, the demonstrated love of Christ is the prototype for building the pastor.

John's vision of the Woman Clothed with the Sun in the book of Revelation gives a clear depiction of how God builds the pastor.

> *And there appeared a great wonder in heaven; a woman clothed with the sun, and the moon under her feet, and upon her head a crown of twelve stars: And she being with child cried, travailing in birth, and pained to be delivered. Rev 12:1-2 (KJV)*

Pastoral Care

Woman clothed with the sun. In the vision, John's sees a woman. A woman is known for compassion and nurture. This is the primary attribute of the pastor. He will look out for the people of God and have a care as a mother does. Paul's words reflect this sort of pastoral care.

> *But we were gentle among you, even as a nurse cherisheth her children: So being affectionately desirous of you, we were willing to have imparted unto you, not the gospel of God only, but also our own souls, because ye were dear unto us. 1 Thess 2:7-8 (KJV)*

God makes this kind of compassion a part of the pastor's spiritual composition. The woman being clothed with the sun represents the pastor's commitment to Christ.

The pastor will wear godliness, holiness, maturity, integrity, strength, wisdom, and grace. He will have the heart of the Father and the very radiance of Christ in his conduct.

Pastoral Wisdom

Moon at her feet. The moon at the woman's feet represents "light in darkness." The pastor has wisdom and insight into the word of God.

The moon shines brightest at night. His ministry of the word will provide light to believers in a dark world.

Thy word is a lamp unto my feet, and a light unto my path. Psalms 119:105 (KJV)

The pastor's insight will help believers make it through the dark times in their lives. His ministry will be a lighthouse to those he leads.

This demonstrates also that the word will be the governing factor of the pastor's life.

He will not only preach the word, but also live by it. The moon at her feet represents the pastor's resolve to allow the light of the word to penetrate any areas of personal darkness within himself.

Pastoral Authority

Crown of twelve stars on head. The twelve stars represent complete authority. The pastor has the full authority of God to lead the people. In addition, he will operate in spiritual authority, which will be characterized by wisdom and grace.

Take heed therefore unto yourselves, and to all the flock, over the which the Holy Ghost hath made you overseers, to feed the church of God, which he hath purchased with his own blood. Acts 20:28 (KJV)

The stars also reflect God's endorsement upon the pastor to have the oversight. God's endorsement should be the "crown" of the pastor's spiritual composition.

Pastoral Burden

Being with Child. The final attribute of the vision of the woman is that she is with child experiencing labor pains. This represents the pastor's continual burden and concern for the people. Though the pastor has to balance this concern by presenting the people to Christ, he will be like the woman.

Bear ye one another's burdens, and so fulfill the law of Christ. Gal 6:2 (KJV)

He will have the welfare and well-being of

the people in his heart and mind, continually. Remember, he is joined (yoked) to the people.

THE BELIEVER'S GUIDE TO THE PASTORL MINISTRY — A Comprehensive Study of the Pastoral Ministry in the Church

-Chapter 4-

The Pastor's Character:

Paul and Timothy

As shepherds, fathers, and watchmen, pastors reveal the nature of Christ and God. The pastor's ministry is not only based upon what they do, but also in who they are. True pastors are known primarily by their godly characters.

Before exploring the functions of the pastor, the pastor's character has to be addressed in detail. Success in ministry depends on quality character and conduct.

A bishop then must be blameless,

the husband of one wife, vigilant, sober, of good behavior, given to hospitality, apt to teach; Not given to wine, no striker, not greedy of filthy lucre; but patient, not a brawler, not covetous; One that ruleth well his own house, having his children in subjection with all gravity; (For if a man know not how to rule his own house, how shall he take care of the church of God?) Not a novice, lest being lifted up with pride he fall into the condemnation of the devil. Moreover he must have a good report of them which are without; lest he fall into reproach and the snare of the devil. (I Timothy 3:2-7)

The pastor's character is outlined in Paul's epistle to Timothy. The word bishop comes from a word meaning overseer. This means the qualifications listed are for those who will take the oversight in the Church, which includes bishops, pastors, and elders alike. True pastors will meet the qualifications listed by Paul.

Blameless

The pastor must be blameless. This does not mean that he is without fault and cannot make mistakes. It does mean that a pastor cannot be known or identified by a known sin.

A bishop then must be blameless...

No one from in or outside of the Church should be able to bring up true slanderous charges against the servant of the Lord. Holiness has to characterize the pastor's life or the ministry in him will be frustrated.

Husband of One Wife

Pastors have to be examples in their personal lives. This exhortation is a direct prohibition against polygamy. Yet, it has a greater implication.

A pastor's personal life has to reflect proper moral conduct that compliments the gospel. Thus, this exhortation speaks to faithfulness in marriage and against any sexual misconduct.

The pastor is not to seek any sexual gratification outside the confines of the marriage bed.

This exhortation reveals the pastor's need for sexual purity. His lifestyle should reflect proper social standards for living.

Vigilant

Pastors have to possess vigilance. Vigilance speaks to the pastor's faithfulness in the execution of the ministry. Every pastor must be faithful to the call of God. He must demonstrate loyalty to Christ and the Church.

> *Let a man so account of us, as of the ministers of Christ, and stewards of the mysteries of God. Moreover it is required in stewards, that a man be found faithful. (I Corinthians 4:1-2)*

Since pastoral ministry is continuous labor, faithfulness will sustain the pastor in times of great struggle. One of God's attributes is faithfulness; therefore, the pastor has to be faithful as he carries out the will of God.

Sober

A pastor has to be sober in judgment and character. Paul is not referring to sobriety in terms of alcohol, but in demonstration and execution of the ministry. Pastors cannot be foolish and immature. They must possess godly, sound wisdom in their lives.

> *For who hath known the mind of the Lord, that he may instruct him? But we have the mind of Christ. (I Corinthians 2:16)*

Pastors should reveal the mind of Christ in their ministries. They have to rely on the wisdom and instruction of the Holy Spirit in the discharging of their duties.

Good Behavior

Pastors are to exhibit good behavior. Pastors have to exercise patience and kindness as they minister to the Church. Pastors are not to be "task masters" over the people of God.

They must exercise patience as they execute their ministries. They have to exercise kindness and faithfulness as they interact with the Body of Christ.

> *For a bishop must be blameless, as the steward of God; not self-willed, not soon angry... (Titus 1: 7)*

Pastors have to know how to conduct themselves as recipients of the grace and mercy of God. With this understanding, their lives at home and among the saints must be in demonstration of the kindness of God.

Given to Hospitality

Every pastor has to be someone who is approachable. Paul exhorted Timothy to look for those who know how to entreat others. Some pastors only interact with believers from the pulpit. However, hospitality is to be demonstrated outside of the location of the Church.

This exhortation does not mean that pastors should not have lives outside of the church. However, it promotes genuine fellowship with others even in their daily lives.

Apt to Teach

Pastors have to be willing to instruct others as the need arises. They ought to understand the foundational truths of the faith and be willing to share with others at all times. They have to be willing to teach with the right attitude also. They must have the right words with the proper delivery. It is a required trait of the servant of the Lord.

> *And the servant of the Lord must not strive; but be gentle unto all men, apt to teach, patient, In meekness instructing those that oppose themselves; if God peradventure will give them repentance to the acknowledging of the truth. (II Timothy 2:24)*

Not given to wine

Pastors should not be under the influence of alcoholic substances. They should not be drunkards. They should not be under the influence of any intoxicating substance, including drugs (prescription or otherwise).

And be not drunk with wine, wherein is excess; but be filled with the Spirit. (Ephesians 5:18)

In addition, pastors should not be under the influence of any intoxicating substance, which includes drugs (illegal or prescription).

Not a striker, Not a brawler

Pastors are not to engage in verbal and physical conflicts. They are not to be argumentative. They are to hold the truth in love. They are not to have bad attitudes and harsh demeanors.

no striker, not greedy of filthy lucre; but patient, not a brawler... (I Timothy 3:3)

Again, they are not to resolve any disputes (professional, personal, and ministerial) with the use of physical violence.

Self-control is needed in the pulpit, on the mission field, or in their homes.

Not Greedy for Money or Covetous

True pastors will not preach and teach for money. They are motivated by a love for the Church and obedience to Christ.

In addition, they will not covet material gain and vain recognition. Pastors should never use their office to become rich. The church is not to be used for personal gain.

This is an area where many pastors fall. They use the exhortation of the scriptures to give as an excuse for greed.

Patient

Patience is one of the identifiable marks of a true pastor. Pastors have to be men of patience as they minister to the Church. Patience is vital for this ministry.

Pastors must have patience as they wait to see the fruits of their labors develop in the lives of believers. They must exercise patience as they their ministries.

Rules own house well

A pastor should know how to lead his family. He should have the respect and support of his wife and children.

The exhortation is simple, if he does not know how to govern his own house; he will be ineffective in the pastoral office.

> *For if a man know not how to rule his own house, how shall he take care of the church of God? (I Timothy 3:5)*

This qualification reveals the pastor's ability to maintain order in the Church. In addition, his example should make it easy for individuals to follow his leadership.

> *Remember them which have the rule over you, who have spoken unto you the word of God: whose faith follow, considering the end of their conversation. (Hebrews 13:7)*

Anyone called to the pastoral ministry must remember that success in ministry is not in ministerial activities, but in the demonstration of the nature of Christ who is the Good Shepherd. Godly character will determine the pastor's effectiveness as a servant of Jesus Christ.

For a full examination of the pastoral ministry, please see my book, **I Will Give You Pastors: Examining the Pastoral Office in the New Testament Church"**

THE BELIEVER'S GUIDE TO THE PASTORL MINISTRY — A Comprehensive Study of the Pastoral Ministry in the Church

-Book 2-

I Will Give You Pastors:

Examining the Pastoral Office in the New Testament Church

God promised Israel godly shepherds. The focus of this book is to bring clarity and understanding to the pastoral office and the pastoral anointing. This information will help individuals to recognize the operations of this anointing in their lives and in the lives of others. It is our hope that believers will develop a greater respect and appreciation for the pastoral office and gift.

THE BELIEVER'S GUIDE TO THE PASTORL MINISTRY   A Comprehensive Study of the Pastoral Ministry in the Church

Introduction

At His departure, Jesus instructed the disciples to go to Jerusalem to await the promise of the Father. On the day of Pentecost, this promise was fulfilled with the outpouring of the Holy Spirit.

The Holy Spirit was given so that the work of Jesus Christ would continue on the earth. The Ministerial Endowments Series is designed to bring clarity to the gifts and ministries given to the Church. It is our prayer that believers will be enlightened and encouraged.

THE BELIEVER'S GUIDE TO THE PASTORL MINISTRY — A Comprehensive Study of the Pastoral Ministry in the Church

In this publication:

God promised Israel godly shepherds. The focus of this book is to bring clarity and understanding to the pastoral office and the pastoral anointing. This information will help individuals to recognize the operations of this anointing in their lives and in the lives of others. It is our hope that believers will develop a greater respect and appreciation for the pastoral office and gift.

-Chapter 1-

What is a Pastor?

The first ministry to be on display in the New Testament Church was that of the apostle. Secondarily, we see the ministry of the prophets and teachers with the apostles with men such as Agabus, Judas, Apollos, and Silas. Further reading shows the ministry of the evangelist was recognized in Philip.

The pastoral ministry developed (last) as Paul and others set elders and leaders over the churches that were established.

Today, we see that there is a shifting in the above model. The pastoral ministry is now the most prevalent and accepted ministry in the Church, while there is debate surrounding the others. Regardless of this phenomenon, pastoral ministry is vital to the furtherance and growth of the Church.

The word pastor originates from the Greek

word poimen, which literally means shepherd. Pastors are given to feed the flock of God, lead them into green pastures, and protect against wolves in sheep's clothing.

Not all pastors will discharge their duty in the same manner; neither will they all have the same anointing. Pastors' ministries will vary in demonstration and execution. Before going into detail concerning the ministry of the pastor, we want to present some foundational truths concerning their ministries.

Pastors are the shepherds and overseers of the people of God. Their title describes their function; they care for the people of God in the Spirit, as a shepherd does sheep. They watch out for the souls of those whom they lead.

Pastors, seemingly, wear more hats than any of the other offices. They have to serve as counselors, preachers, teachers, intercessors, mediators, and the like. Consider now other points about the pastoral office:

The Facts of Pastoral Ministry

Pastors cause the people of God to grow/prosper through their ministry. They do this through their ministry of the Word. Their congregants should be able to feed and mature.

> *And I will set up shepherds over them which shall feed them: and they shall fear no more, nor be dismayed, neither shall they be lacking, saith the Lord. (Jeremiah 23:4)*

Pastors lead by instruction and example. We must follow. Along with the ministry of the Word, pastors must be examples. A natural shepherd does more leading than talking. Even if the pastor has not said one word, the people of God should see the Word demonstrated in his lifestyle.

> *Remember them, which have the rule over you, who have spoken the word of God: whose faith follow, considering the end of the conversation. (Hebrews 13:7)*

Pastors are to represent the heart of God and care for the Church. Pastors should take on the nature of the Good Shepherd. They are protectors over the flock of God as watchmen.

> *And I will give you pastors after mine own heart, which shall feed you with knowledge and understanding. (Jeremiah 3:15)*

Pastors must guard against the Pharisaic spirit: preaching and teaching only for the praise of men. They have to remember they are privileged to lead.

They must not look upon the people of God as their servants, but rather be ready to serve. In doing so, they and the people of God will grow into the fullness of the stature of Christ.

The Function of Pastoral Ministry

Every pastor is unique in his ministry. However, the pastor's role in the kingdom of God directly parallels a shepherd's role. Some of God's chief servants were first shepherds. Abel, Moses, David, and Amos were shepherds.

The 23rd Psalm depicts how God as the Shepherd cares for His people. Yet, this Psalm reveals how the New Testament pastor functions in the Church.

Shepherds provide for the sheep. David

began the psalm by stating that he did not lack anything because the Lord was his shepherd. A natural shepherd makes provision for the sheep. He ensures they have what they need for survival.

The Lord is my shepherd; I shall not want. (Psalm 23:1)

Pastors will endeavor to provide the saints with what they need to live a victorious Christian life. God set pastors in the Church to reveal the love and comfort of the Good Shepherd.

Shepherds feed the flock with wisdom and knowledge. A natural shepherd leads the flock to places where they can be nourished with food and water. The pastor, through his ministry of the Word, provides people with knowledge of God and His ways.

> *He maketh me to lie down in green pastures: he leadeth me beside the still waters. (Psalm 23:2)*

Therefore, pastors have to endeavor to preach sound doctrine only. They have to avoid preaching messages that compromise the truth of the gospel.

Shepherds correct and comfort the sheep of the fold. A natural shepherd carries a rod and staff. The staff is designed to keep the flock together, while the rod is designed to bring a sheep back into the fold when it runs away.

> *...thy rod and thy staff they comfort me. (Psalm 23:4b*

A pastor has to correct individuals who are rebellious and disobedient. However, rebukes that are administered have to be given for the salvation of the individual and not the embarrassment. God rebukes because of love, not out of frustration. The pastor has to do the same.

> *As many as I love, I rebuke and chasten: be zealous therefore, and repent. (Revelation 3:19)*

After the word of rebuke and correction comes from the pastor, he then has to be willing to comfort and restore. God delights in restoration and repentance. The pastor has to demonstrate this in ministry.

> *Brethren, if a man be overtaken in a fault, ye which are spiritual, restore such an one in the spirit of meekness; considering thyself, lest thou also be tempted. Bear ye one another's burdens, and so fulfill the law of*

> *Christ. (Galatians 6:1-2)*

Shepherds protect the flock. A natural shepherd protects the sheep against wolves and thieves. He is willing to put in his life in jeopardy for the lives of the sheep.

> *I am the good shepherd: the good shepherd giveth his life for the sheep. (John 10:11)*

Pastors give believers strategies for overcoming spiritual attacks of the adversary. In addition, they expose and reveal false ministers who want to fleece the flock.

The Focus of Pastoral Ministry

Pastors in their ministries endeavor to reveal the personality of God to the Church. They reflect the nature of the Good Shepherd. They have a love for God and strive to make others aware of the love of God towards them.

They have fatherly concern and love for the members of the Body of Christ. Pastors will know how to express the innermost heart of God and bring people into a father-child relationship with the Lord. At the core, pastors want to see men and women be conformed to the likeness and image of Christ.

The heart of God from the beginning was to have sons and daughters. The pastoral ministry is given to help others see God as their Father; ultimately resulting in the eternal salvation of those who receive their ministries.

Now, that we have discussed some elementary truths concerning the pastoral ministry, we will now look at the call of the pastor.

THE BELIEVER'S GUIDE TO THE PASTORL MINISTRY — A Comprehensive Study of the Pastoral Ministry in the Church

-Chapter 2-

The Call of a Pastor

God calls individuals to the pastoral office in many ways. In the Old and New Testaments, we discover that God called men in different manners. God's call to the pastoral office is an honorable call.

The pastor's ministry is needed if the Church is going to mature and the people of God remain in Christ. Therefore, God has to establish the one called to this ministry through how He calls them.

There are individuals who occupy the office of the pastor without having a commission for the Lord. Always remember that a desire to pastor is not a call to pastorate.

This chapter is designed to help believers recognize the pastoral calling upon others and themselves. We will look at scriptural examples of how the Lord called individuals to understand the call of the pastor.

Perceiving the Pastoral Call

The call of a pastor is unique from others in one respect. Though all ministers receive their calling from the Lord, the pastoral call comes with a direct charge to connect with God's people.

One is not a pastor because he teaches and preaches. There has to be a connection and love for God's people intertwined with his ability to minister. Else, the pastor will not be a pastor, but a teacher. Since the New Testament introduces us to the ministry of the pastor, we will use two main examples from these texts to understand the pastor's call.

Jesus & Peter

After the crucifixion and resurrection of

Jesus, He appears to the disciples. He then calls Peter aside to give him a personal commission. This reveals that those called to the pastorate will have a personal commission of Christ accompanied by confirmation within the Body.

> *So when they had dined, Jesus saith to Simon Peter, Simon, son of Jonas, lovest thou me more than these? He saith unto him, Yea, Lord; thou knowest that I love thee. He saith unto him, Feed my lambs. John 21:15 (KJV)*

Jesus' commission of Peter was inseparable with Peter's responsibility to the Church. He was to feed the people as a shepherd feeds his flock. Jesus calls His followers, lambs. It is a term of endearment revealing His tender care. This same care must be demonstrated in those called to the pastorate.

Before Jesus commissioned Peter, He questions the level of Peter's love for Him. Anyone called to pastor must love Christ more than the work of the ministry. If the one called loves Christ, he will undoubtedly love the people since they are Christ's Body. Peter's commission of Christ demonstrates that every pastor will have a personal, definite call of Christ.

Though the Church may place people in positions of authority, true spiritual authority comes from Christ. If you feel you are called to pastor, you will have a definite revelation of Christ concerning this.

Paul & Titus

Though the pastor must have a personal call

from Christ, God may use others in leadership to verify the call and initiate one's entrance into pastoral ministry.

We discover from the scriptures that Titus accompanied Paul during his ministry. Undoubtedly, Paul instructed Titus as his own son in the ministry. While imprisoned and laboring in other areas, Paul sent Titus to exercise oversight in certain churches during his absence.

We see, then, that Titus' entrance into the pastoral was through leadership, according to the will of God. Consider Paul's words to the Corinthians,

> *I desired Titus, and with him I sent a brother. Did Titus make a gain of you? walked we not in the same spirit? walked we not in the same steps? 2 Cor 12:18 (KJV)*

Paul sent Titus to exercise pastoral oversight through his apostolic authority. We see the providence of God in action in propelling him into pastoral ministry. This same is true today. Remember, the call to pastor has to be personal and confirmed within the Body.

Preparing for the Pastoral Call

Once an individual receives a call to the pastoral office, there must be a response and answer to the Lord. Before the pastor's making (discussed in the next chapter) begins, there are certain things that the future pastor has to do.

Seek Submission

The pastor's office comes with great authority. He will be responsible for the souls entrusted to him. Therefore, the pastor has to guard his spirit against arrogance, pride, and totalitarianism. A sure of way of this is to develop a servant's heart. He should seek opportunities to serve.

If he expects others to submit to his authority, he has to learn what it means to be in submission to another. This will help him not to abuse the authority given to him by Christ.

But he that is greatest among you shall be your servant. (Matthew 23:11)

Some individuals receive a call to the pastoral office after being in ministry for years. In this instance, individuals need to increase how they serve and their demonstration of submission for the coming pastoral ministry. Jesus demonstrated the level of submission that a pastor needs as He recounted His connection to the Father.

I can of mine own self do nothing: as I hear, I judge: and my judgment is just; because I seek not mine own will, but the will of the Father which hath sent me. John 5:30 (KJV)

Jesus showed the people that even though He came from God, He was in submission. This is important to any pastor since they may operate in ministry without tangible accountability at times. Hence, a submissive spirit will keep them from spiritual pride.

Seek Solitude

After perceiving a call to the pastorate, a time of separation is needed to ensure the pastor's success. The separation does not necessarily have to be physical, but definitely spiritual.

The future pastor has to take time to seek

the Lord and receive specific instructions as to how he should execute his ministry. After his conversion and calling, Paul experienced a time of separation in order to be instructed of the Lord.

> *But when it pleased God, who separated me from my mother's womb, and called me by his grace, To reveal his Son in me, that I might preach him among the heathen; immediately I conferred not with flesh and blood: Neither went I up to Jerusalem to them which were apostles before me; but I went into Arabia, and returned again unto Damascus. Then after three years I went up to Jerusalem to see Peter, and abode with him fifteen days. (Galatians 1:15-18)*

Paul wrote that when God wanted to reveal

Christ to him, he went into Arabia and then Damascus over the space of three years. He wrote that he did not discuss it with men, he allowed the Lord to minister unto him.

After the Lord was finished, Paul spoke to other leaders to verify the things he had received. This denotes that future pastors should seek for godly wisdom and counsel as they enter into their ministries.

Seek Sanctification

A call to the pastoral office is an invitation to spiritual warfare and temptation. If the enemy cannot stop the individual's resolve to serve the Lord, he will weaken the future pastor's ministry through ungodliness. Therefore, the pastoral candidate has to seek sanctification; that is, a life of holiness to ensure success in the ministry.

But I keep under my body, and bring it into subjection: lest that by any means, when I have preached to others, I myself should be a castaway. (I Corinthians 9:27)

Paul, after years of ministry, confessed that he still had to bring his body (flesh and its lusts) under subjection. The pastor's quest for holiness augments at the reception of his calling and develops during its fulfillment. His quest should become greater because of the continual interaction with others which could prove challenging.

Performing the Pastoral Call

Since the pastoral office is very solemn and serious, reflecting the nature of Christ; we must be certain and clear in recognizing and accepting the pastoral calling in our lives and in the lives of others. Therefore, in concluding our examination of the call of a pastor, we will discuss briefly certain signs of the pastoral calling This will help in the acceptance of the pastoral call on an individual's life.

Love of Jesus Christ

The individual who is called to then pastoral office will have a profound love for God and Christ. He will speak of Christ in the most personal terms. He will also have a love and deeply personal concern for others in the Body of Christ.

We have already stated that Peter's personal commission was accompanied by an acknowledgement of how he felt about Christ. We must remember, however, that all believers are to love Christ and the Church. God will impart a deep compassion to those called so that they will care for the house of God as they would their own families.

Though the pastor will have this level of love and compassion, any believer is a candidate for it. Again, this is given as a sign of a call to the pastoral office.

Consistent Intercession

Pastors, again, will have a deep love for Christ and the Church. Because of this, those who are called to this office will have consistent prayer lives. Much of their prayer will be for the Church, its members, and its advancement. They have a desire to see Christ formed in those whom they oversee.

In his letters, the apostle Paul would tell the churches of his constant intercession for them. He told the Galatians that he would labor (which includes prayer) so that Christ would be formed in them.

> *My little children, of whom I travail in birth again until Christ be formed in you...Gal 4:19 (KJV)*

Conversely, we know that Jesus challenges all believers to be consistent in prayer. In addition, the scriptures continually admonish believers to be intercessors for one another. Again, consistent intercession may be a sign of the pastoral office, not the manifestation of it.

Authority in the Spirit

One of the sure signs of a pastoral call is the presence of great authority in the Spirit. Those who called to the pastoral office will command the respect of those that are around them.

Additionally, they have the gifts of the

Spirit operating in them consistently. This is to equip them fully for pastoral service. God will make them able ministers of the New Testament.

Who also hath made us able ministers of the new testament; not of the letter, but of the spirit: for the letter killeth, but the spirit giveth life. 2 Cor 3:6 (KJV)

Keep in mind, however, that the revelation and power of the Spirit is available to all Christians. Jesus said that miraculous signs would follow anyone who believed on Him. Therefore, it is not uncommon to see believers who are not called to the pastoral office possessing great power and authority.

The presence of power and authority, again, is only a sign of the pastoral call. We have already established that PASTORS MUST HAVE A PERSONAL COMMISSION FROM CHRIST. The above signs are only indications of a pastoral call.

Once a pastoral call is established, the pastor goes through training and discipline. In the next chapter, we will discuss the making of a pastor. Exercising great power and authority in the Spirit and oversight of God's people is not the hallmark of the pastor's ministry; it is his character. Therefore, Christ builds the pastor to reflect His nature.

-Chapter 3-

The Office of the Pastor

So the last shall be first, and the first last...

(Matthew 20:16)

Though there are varieties of ministries and operations, pastors have essentially the same functions. Some functions are not exclusive to pastors. However, pastors will differ from other ministries in the execution of those functions.

NINE FUNCTIONS OF THE PASTORAL OFFICE

Preach & Teach the Word of God (I Tim. 2:7). Pastors are gifted to preach and/or teach the word of God under divine inspiration. They have the ability to mature believers in the Word of God. They are anointed to ground the believers in foundational truths of the kingdom. This is performed with godly character and wisdom.

> *And I will give you pastors according to mine heart, which shall feed you with knowledge and understanding. (Jeremiah 3:15)*

Release Believers into their Spiritual Gifts (Acts 8:17; Romans 1:11; II Tim. 1:6). Pastors have the ability to bring forth the gifts of God in believers. They have the responsibility to ensure that believers use their gifts effectively in God's service.

Pastors, through the Spirit's direction, will steer believers into their areas of gifting and ministry. They help to stir up gifts in believers through the laying on of hands.

> *Neglect not the gift that is in thee, which was given thee by prophecy, with the laying on of The hands of the presbytery. (I Timothy 4:14)*

Establish and/or Oversee the Local Church. Because pastors are shepherds, they are most effective with the flock. Therefore, some pastors will begin new ministries to fulfill their ministries while others will take the oversight of existing churches.

As the leader of the local church, the pastor (or senior pastor in some cases) is responsible for the spiritual direction and protection of the flock given to him by God.

Unto the angel of the church...

write... (Revelation 2:1)

In the book of Revelation, Jesus gave John prophetic words to be given to the pastors (angels) of the local assemblies. It was their responsibility to ensure that the people responded to God's word.

Serve as Intercessors. Pastoral ministry resembles the priestly ministry in this area. They will stand before God on the needs of those entrusted to them.

They desire to see the saints grow and prosper as they serve the Lord. Prayer will be a definite hallmark of the pastoral ministry.

> *We then that are strong ought to bear the infirmities of the weak, and not to please ourselves. (Romans 15:1)*

Train Leaders (Acts 15:39; II Tim. 2:1-2; Acts 6:3-6). Because of their positions in the Church, pastors have the responsibility to train future leaders. Though these leaders may have different callings, pastors have to create an atmosphere that other leaders will learn to operate in their gifts and ministries.

To Titus, mine own son after the common faith: Grace, mercy, and peace, from God the Father and the Lord Jesus Christ our Saviour. For this cause left I thee in Crete, that thou shouldest set in order the things that are wanting, and ordain elders in every city, as I had appointed thee. (Titus 1:4-5)

Expose False Ministers & Doctrine. As watchmen, pastors have the gifting and responsibility to inform saints of deceptive doctrines and ministers. They will contend for purity of faith and doctrine in the Church. They, like the prophets of old, will warn and speak against false ministers openly.

But there were false prophets also among the people, even as there shall be false teachers among you, who privily shall bring in damnable heresies, even denying the Lord that bought them, and bring upon themselves swift destruction. And many shall follow their pernicious ways; by reason of whom the way of truth shall be evil spoken of. (II Peter 2:1-2)

Perform Signs, Wonders, Healings, & Miracles. Though the pastor's main function is to shepherd God's people, they will have the power of God to confirm their message. Pastors will have the gifts of the Spirit operating in their ministries. Without His power and revelation, the pastor will not be truly effective.

And fear came upon every soul; and many wonders and signs were done by the apostles. (Acts 2:43)

Serve as Counselors. Because the pastoral is a stationary ministry, they will be personally involved in the believer's life.

Due to this fact, they are called upon to offer counsel to their followers. Thus, God endows pastors with the spirit of wisdom and counsel that the people will make sound, godly decisions in their lives.

> And the spirit of the Lord shall rest upon him, the spirit of wisdom and understanding, the spirit of counsel and might, the spirit of knowledge

and of the fear of the Lord. (Isaiah 11:2)

Establish Believers in the Faith. Pastors have the task of establishing people in the faith. This is so believers will not follow false doctrines and ministers. The messages that they preach and teach with the godly wisdom imparted from the Lord produces mature and solid saints.

In addition, they are able to instruct babes in Christ until they become mature in their personal relationships with God and in their doctrinal beliefs. They can promote stability and growth in the Body of Christ. Though there are many other functions fulfilled in the pastoral ministry, most pastors will demonstrate these functions at some time in their ministries.

THE FOCUS OF PASTORAL MINISTRY

The pastoral ministry is governed by two focal points.

Reveal God's Personality

Pastors in their ministries endeavor to reveal the personality of

God to the Church. They reflect the nature of the Good Shepherd. They have a love for God and strive to make others aware of the love of God towards them.

They have fatherly concern and love for the members of the Body of Christ. Pastors will know how to express the innermost heart of God and bring people into a father-child relationship with the Lord.

Conformity of the Christian

At the core, pastors want to see

men and women be conformed to the likeness and image of Christ.

The heart of God from the beginning was to have sons and daughters. The pastoral ministry is given to help others see God as their Father; ultimately resulting in the eternal salvation of those who receive their ministries.

-Chapter 4-

The Roles of Pastors

Shepherding is the defining mark of the pastoral ministry though pastoral ministries will vary in demonstration and execution.

We must remember the following exhortation of scripture when considering the work of God in all the ministries.

> *Now there are diversities of gifts, but the same Spirit. And there are differences of administrations, but the same Lord. And there are diversities of operations, but it is the same God which worketh all*

in all. (I Corinthians 12:4-6)

Pastoral ministry manifests itself in various ways. However, there is some common ground among all pastors.

No matter what their specific call is, pastors will (in addition to acting as shepherds) exhibit characteristics of fathers and watchmen as they minister in the Church.

PASTORS AS FATHERS

The role of a pastor in the Church is not only to be a shepherd (discussed in chapter 1), but also to serve as a "father" ministry (like the apostle). The pastor's role in the kingdom (like that of the apostle) is similar to that of a father.

The apostles, themselves, referred to themselves as fathers and to those who partook of their ministry as their children. While writing to the Corinthian church, Paul likened his ministry unto a father. John called the saints his children.

> *For if you were to have countless tutors in Christ, yet you would not have many fathers; for in Christ Jesus, I became your father through*

the gospel. (I Corinthians 4:15 NASV)

My little children, these things write I unto you, that ye sin not. And if any man sin, we have an advocate with the Father, Jesus Christ the righteous. (I John 2:1)

The pastor will love the Church as a father loves his children. His personality in the Church will resemble that of a father.

Fathers provide for their children. As an earthly father provides for the needs of his children, the pastor will supply the spiritual needs of those entrusted to him. He will endeavor to ensure that the Church has the right information to live in this world in victory.

They will strive to lay proper foundations in the lives of the people of God; that they may inherit the kingdom of God. Paul wrote,

> *Behold, the third time I am ready to come to you; and I will not be burdensome to you: for I seek not yours, but you: for the children ought not to lay up for the parents,*

but the parents for the children. And I will very gladly spend and be spent for you; though the more abundantly I love you, the less I be loved. (II Corinthians 12:14-15)

He explained to those at Corinth that as a father works and provides (spends) for his children, so he labors and expends his time, energy, and effort to provide for them spiritually. He wanted their souls to be saved.

Pastors have to avoid becoming "lord" and "kings" over the people of God.

God has set them in the Church to serve.

Fathers nurture their children. Though a father provides for his children, provision without nurture handicaps a child. A pastor must not only labor in the Church, his labor has to be come from genuine concern.

Whatever the pastor's specific strength in ministry is, his concern will be a personal one.

> *But I (Paul and other apostles) proved to be gentle among you, as a nursing mother tenderly cares for her*

own children.n (I Thessalonians 2:7 NASV, Parenthesis mine)

The pastor's personal concern has to be tempered with grace and patience. Because God uses them to rebuke and correct, some pastors become harsh in their words and demeanor. The anointing of God is not to be blamed for character flaws.

Fathers discipline their children. If a child has no discipline or training, he is liable to develop into a corrupt adult. The same is true for believers. If Christians are not disciplined, they will not grow up into mature saints.

Pastors will execute discipline in the Church. However, love is to be the motivation for the rebuke. John demonstrated this pastoral responsibility in his third epistle.

> *For this reason, if I come, I will call attention to his deeds which he does, unjustly accusing us with the wicked words; and not satisfied with this, neither does he himself receive the brethren, and he forbid those who*

desire to do so, and puts them out of the Church. (III John verse 10 NASV)

John says that he will "call attention" to what a divisive minister did. He was expressing that he would personally deal with the individual because of his error. Paul, on numerous occasions, exercised meted out discipline in the Church.

While away from Corinth, news reached him that a brother was sleeping with this stepmother. He not only rebuked the church for not handling the situation, but also gave instruction concerning the discipline of the brother.

It is reported commonly that there is fornication among you, and such fornication as is not so much as named among the Gentiles, that one should have his father's wife. And ye are puffed up, and have not rather mourned, that he that hath done this deed might be taken away from among you. For I verily, as absent in body, but present in spirit, have judged already, as though I were present, concerning him that hath so done this deed, In the name of our Lord Jesus Christ, when ye are gathered together, and my spirit, with the power of our Lord Jesus Christ, To deliver such an one unto Satan for the destruction of the flesh, that the spirit may be saved in the day of the Lord Jesus. (I Corinthians 5:1-5)

Paul meted out discipline. However, it was for the salvation of the offender. True fathers discipline their children to save them. When a pastor rebukes, it has to be done in love, else he will offend one of God's very own. He must remember that he has a Father in heaven.

Fathers give wise/sound instruction to their children. The book of Proverbs is a compilation of instructions that a father would give to his children.

Fathers seek to instill knowledge in their children. A father will pass on the information that he has learned.

Pastors will impart revelation and

knowledge to the Church as a father does to his children.

And I will give you pastors according to mine heart, which shall feed you with knowledge and understanding. (Jeremiah 3:15)

Pastors are to preach undefiled sermons and impart the wisdom that comes from God to believers. Pastors are expected to give fatherly wisdom and instruction in the Church.

PASTORS AS WATCHMEN

Pastors fulfill many functions in

Body of Christ. One of the important roles is that of watchmen. We know that watchmen would be placed in strategic locations to warn towns, cities, and countries of impending attack. Pastors function in a similar manner.

Yet, the pastoral watchman has an additional role in this duty. He also watches over the souls of those that are entrusted to him. God's command to Ezekiel the prophet reveals the pastor's role as watchman.

Watchmen warn against danger. An

earthly watchman warns against ensuing disaster and danger. The pastor has to reveal spiritual attacks that will come to the Church and God's displeasure in the Church.

> *Son of man, I have made thee a watchman unto the house of Israel: therefore hear the word at my mouth, and give them warning from me. (Ezekiel 3:17)*

The pastor has to warn the people to prepare themselves for warfare. In addition, he warns the people that they may turn from sin to please God.

Watchmen oversee the activities of those under their supervision. Watchmen not only have to warn against external threats, but also internal threats. The watchman reveals dangers and disasters within the territory.

The pastor has to do the same. He serves as a watchman over the people of God. He reveals weaknesses in the Church.

The Pastoral Watchman oversees the souls of the believers. The pastor is concerned with the spiritual progress of the souls of the believers. In his epistle, John expressed this pastoral concern.

> *Beloved, I wish above all things that thou mayest prosper and be in health, even as thy soul prospereth. (3 John verse 2)*

John expressed his desire for the natural and spiritual prosperity of the saints. As the Good Shepherd restores the soul, the pastor will strive to bring healing and wholeness to the soul of the believer.

He will help them to work through

personal conflicts and frustrations that they may walk in the fullness of the gospel of Jesus Christ.

For a discussion on the person who has a pastoral gift while not occupying the pastoral office, please see my book, "The Perfecting of the Pastoral Person: The Preparation of the Pastoral Person for Ministry and Service."

-Chapter 5-

False Pastors

There is still much to be learned about the pastoral anointing. However, understanding comes with responsibility. God is setting a new standard for all ministers, ministries, and laymen to follow. The Church has to stand against deception. The scriptures are clear that the number of false ministers will increase as the end of this age approaches.

Not every individual preaching in the name of the Lord is His servant. The enemy seeks to destroy the work of God in the earth through imitation. Therefore, the enemy sets his false ministers in the Church to undermine the work of God's chosen vessels.

False ministers are here, but the saints are not to be afraid of falling into deception. False ministers provide a service to the Church. How?

For there must be also heresies among

you, that they which are approved may be made manifest among you. (I Corinthians 11:19)

When Paul used the word heresies, he was speaking of divisions and those that caused them. False ministers seek to keep the Church in perpetual dissension and division. Their ministries put enmity between believers with the intent to create a following for themselves.

The answer to "How do false ministers provide a service to the Church?" seems non-existent. However, the statement of Paul provides a simple explanation.

False ministers help us to recognize true ministers of God. Paul said that there must be heresies (and those that cause them) among you so that those who are approved (right, true, anointed, etc.) might be made visible.

The ministries of false ministers demonstrate to the Church the improper way to minister. Therefore, when true ministry is in operation, it can be received without fear.

CHARACTERISTICS OF FALSE MINISTERS

We cannot end our discussion of pastors without talking about false pastors. Before examining false pastors exclusively, it is imperative that we are able to recognize the characteristics of any false minister (or layman). Jesus gave this warning concerning false ministers.

> *Beware of false prophets, which come to you in sheep's clothing, but inwardly they are ravening wolves. Ye shall know them by their fruits. Do men gather grapes of thorns, or figs of thistles? Even so every good tree bringeth forth good fruit; but a corrupt tree bringeth forth evil fruit. A good*

tree cannot bring forth evil fruit, neither can a corrupt tree bring forth good fruit. Every tree that bringeth not forth good fruit is hewn down, and cast into the fire. Wherefore by their fruits ye shall know them. (Matthew 7:15-20)

One true way to recognize false ministers is by the fruit that they bear. Fruit refers to their lifestyles and not their ministries. Moreover, not everyone that is false calls himself an apostle or prophet.

Though false apostles and prophets exist, there are also false evangelists, pastors, and teachers. Regardless of the title that a false minister has, he (or she) will exhibit the following characteristics.

They preach that godliness is gain. Godliness to false ministers means prosperity and healing.

They seldom teach against sin. They promote serving God for what you can get.

> *If any man teach otherwise, and consent not to wholesome words, even the words of our Lord Jesus Christ, and to the doctrine which is according to godliness; He is proud, knowing nothing, but doting about questions and strifes of words, whereof cometh envy, strife, railings, evil surmisings, perverse disputings of men of corrupt minds, and destitute of the truth, supposing that gain is godliness: from such withdraw thyself. (I Timothy 6:3-5)*

They only teach that you belong to God and should have the best. They promote the concept that God only wants you blessed, without declaring that God also wants character, integrity, and holiness in His people.

Their doctrine focuses on the miraculous work of God and His blessings, exclusively. They promote God's blessing, rather than God and His Christ. They teach individuals how to prosper in God without living for Him.

They were once servants of God. Many false ministers have genuine conversion experiences. They entered ministry by the call of God. However, consistent rebellion, sin, pride, and greed caused them to error from the truth.

> *For if after they have escaped the pollutions of the world through the knowledge of the Lord and Saviour Jesus Christ, they are again entangled therein, and overcome, the latter end is worse with them than the beginning. For it had been better for them not to have known the way of righteousness, than, after they*

have known it, to turn from the holy commandment delivered unto them. But it is happened unto them according to the true proverb, the dog is turned to his own vomit again; and the sow that was washed to her wallowing in the mire. (II Peter 2:20-22)

Peter wrote that false ministers did escape the pollutions of the world by Christ. However, they returned to their sins and filthy ways. Consequently, Peter added, they are worse than they were before their initial conversion. It serves as a warning to every minister. If the love of money, pride, and sin are not rejected, the road to becoming an enemy of God becomes inevitable.

CHARACTERISTICS OF FALSE PASTORS

False pastors will demonstrate the same

behavior as other false ministers. However, there will be certain traits that are readily visible in false pastoral ministers.

They operate in false authority. False pastors do not operate in godly authority. They establish their own authority in the Body of Christ. They disguise their wickedness by first appearing as true pastors.

> *For such are false apostles, deceitful workers, transforming themselves into the apostles of Christ. And no marvel; for Satan himself is transformed into an angel of light. Therefore it is no great thing if his ministers also be transformed as the ministers of righteousness; whose end shall be according to their works. (II Corinthians 11:13-15)*

Paul stated that those who are false would resemble those who are true. However, once they have gained some respect, they will attack other leaders. The false apostles and leaders of Paul's day tried to defame him and establish their own authority in the churches. False pastors use this tactic today. Through the defamation of others, they exalt their personal ministries.

Another tactic used is misinterpretation of scripture to establish authority. They find scriptures that refer to ministerial authority and claim it for themselves. They promote themselves to the offices of the apostle or prophet to give credence to their ministries. They try to walk in the calling of others, which turns into manipulation and deception.

True pastors will be humble men and women with a servant's heart. They will not promote their personal ministries. The authority that they operate in is backed by the power of

God and is recognized in the Church.

They operate in counterfeit gifts. False pastors minister with the wrong motives. Therefore, the Spirit of God withdraws Himself from their ministries. Since false pastors want to appear spiritual, they strive to operate in 'gifts' to validate the ministry.

They begin to rely on their own human spirit and help from demonic influence to appear spiritual. This happened to King Saul.

> *But the Spirit of the Lord departed from Saul, and an evil spirit from the Lord troubled him. (I Samuel 16:14)*

> *And it came to pass on the morrow, that the evil spirit from God came upon Saul, and he prophesied in the midst of the house: and David played with his hand, as at other*

times: and there was a javelin in Saul's hand. (I Samuel 18:10)

Because of Saul's continual rebellion, the Spirit of God departed from him. An evil spirit replaced God's Spirit. When the evil spirit came upon him, he prophesied. His prophecy came from the wrong source. This eventually happens to false pastors. The Holy Spirit lifts and they use demonic influence to still function.

They twist the scriptures. Another tactic used is misinterpretation of scripture to establish authority. They find scriptures that refer to pastoral authority and claim it for themselves. They scare believers into thinking that because they are pastors, they are superior to others.

They possess a controlling spirit. False pastors will use manipulation to gain followers. Once people begin to follow them, they scare the individuals into staying and/or following them. They tell individuals that if they discontinue fellowship with them or their ministries, God will not be pleased and the like.

In addition, false pastors will try to control the people's personal lives. By using false authority, they will tell people who they can marry and where to work. False pastors operate in a similar fashion to cult leaders.

Though false pastors, teachers, and ministers exist, believers are not to walk in fear. However, Christians have to be able to learn to recognize false ministers. In addition, the presence of false ministers should give believers a greater appreciation for godly leaders and ministries within the Church.

THE BELIEVER'S GUIDE TO THE PASTORL MINISTRY — A Comprehensive Study of the Pastoral Ministry in the Church

-Book 3-

Keys to Pastoral Ministry and Recovery:

Help for Wounded Healers

In this issue, we will discuss the need for ministry among pastors and leaders. Jesus was referred to as the Wounded Healer. In spite of rejection and sorrow, He ministered to the needs of others. Today, we find leaders throughout the Body of Christ who are wounded healers. They minister to others without receiving ministry themselves. This has caused many leaders to suffer burn-outs, sicknesses, and even early deaths. In this issue, we want to briefly examine the influences surrounding this problem in leadership.

Introduction

God anoints and endows individuals with gifts and talents to serve in the Church. However, some have missed the very purpose of gifts and ministries in the Church. In the Abundant Truth Leadership Series, we will endeavor to present a proper foundation for believers to minister upon.

In this publication

In this issue, we want to examine the influences surrounding this problem in leadership. We will discuss the reasons why pastors and leaders do not receive needed ministry. In addition, we will explore steps that leaders can employ to receive the help that they need.

It is our prayer that those who minister will be blessed and strengthened from the information presented.

THE BELIEVER'S GUIDE TO THE PASTORL MINISTRY — A Comprehensive Study of the Pastoral Ministry in the Church

-Chapter 1-

PROLOGUE:
The Lysterian Legacy

"We also are men of like passions with you and preach unto you that ye should turn from these vanities unto the living God." (Acts 14:15)

After a man of Lystra received healing, the people wanted to worship the apostles, Paul and Barnabas, and offer sacrifices to them. Barnabas and Paul said,

> *"We also are men of like passions with you and preach unto you that ye should turn from these vanities unto the living God."* (Acts 14:15)

Deification of Leaders

This same scenario is demonstrated even in today's churches. Parishioners deify pastors and church leaders. They hear them present powerful and stirring messages about Jesus Christ and the Christian Faith. The church leaders, to them, seemingly are unaffected by the evils of today.

Therefore, some believe that pastors and other leaders have moved beyond this world and its problems. However, this is simply not true.

In spite of publicized church scandals involving clergy, pastors and leaders are still expected to be perfect and without issues.

It then becomes difficult for a pastor or leader with sins, weaknesses, and problems to receive help. In addition, past scandals involving well-known ministers and denominations have only managed to create fear among leaders.

Reluctancy of Leaders

As a result, many leaders will not seek help without the fear of negative repercussions. However, scandals of the past and present should provoke a pursuit of accountability, integrity, and purity among the clergy. Pastors and other leaders need assistance, as does every Christian.

Parishioners have to understand that their leaders are human while understanding that the calling upon their lives demands a greater level of sacrifice and service. If parishioners have problems and struggles, their leaders will have them also.

However, pastors and leaders have to overcome internal and external influences if they are to receive assistance.

-Chapter 2-
The David Dilemma

The woman conceived and sent word to David, saying, "I am pregnant." (II Samuel 11:5 NIV)

In the book of 2 Samuel, chapter 11, the account of David's adultery with Bathsheba is recorded. In this well-known story, we see that David was in a dilemma as to what he should do after discovering that Bathsheba was pregnant.

The woman conceived and sent word to David, saying, "I am pregnant." (II Samuel 11:5 NIV)

David's dilemma led him to make the horrific choice of devising a scheme to kill Bathsheba's husband to cover his sin. The Bible does not tell us specifically why David chose this extreme course of action.

He knew that God was merciful and would not leave him. However, due to his personal motivations, he would not simply face his sin, but multiplied it.

If he had sought true forgiveness from the Lord and faced the consequences of his actions,

his godly legacy may have been spotted by adultery, but not compounded by deceit, scheming, and abuse of power
to commit murder.

Pastors and leaders today are faced with a dilemma as to how should they receive help for public and personal downfalls, mistakes, and sins. David did not seek help, but the modern pastor and leader should not follow David's legacy.

Again, though David's personal motivations were not elucidated, we will not look at reasons why today's leaders do not receive help, which could lead to greater sin and downfall.

Reasons Why Leaders Don't Receive Help

The most common factors that hinder leaders. from receiving help are pride, embarrassment, hopelessness, ministry security, and family.

These influences can be placed in two categories: Emotional and Social. Until these influences are removed, leaders will continue to minister while they need ministry.

Emotional Influences

Pride. Pastors and leaders are afraid to appear vulnerable, less spiritual, or "human." They will not admit that they have a problem because they are supposed to lead. Therefore, leaders believe that to display any signs of imperfection indicate a lack of spirituality or maturity to other clergy or laity.

Embarrassment. Fear and feelings of embarrassment have the ability to the pursuit for assistance. If the sin is considered highly immoral, leaders are liable to be selective about what they share. Embarrassment grips the mind and heart producing paranoia and guilt as they share feelings.

In turn, personal feelings of embarrassment are transferred onto others. So that, when they speak to anyone concerning their problems, any reaction perceived to be negative or judgmental will stop the quest for help.

Hopelessness. Hopelessness is the silent prison that takes certain leaders captive. They preach and give advice, even though they have lost hope in God and themselves. They minister out of routine, not expecting any results in their own personal lives.

Some ministers develop the attitude, "I am a minister, I should have the answer for my own problems," or "I have tried all that I know and it has not worked."

Therefore, depression, guilt, and unbelief seize their emotions producing doubt. They began to descend into the pit of hopelessness. In this mindset, the reception of counsel and support is frustrated.

Social Influences

Now we will turn attention to the social influences which hinder pastors and leaders from seeking and receiving help.

Security. Some pastors and leaders do not admit they need help for ministry security. Various religious organizations choose their ministers by the vote or interview rather than by the appointment of denominational leaders.

Leaders are chosen by perception rather than reality. Therefore, they feel pressured into keeping personal issues hidden for fear of losing an appointment or position. Though the Church is supposed to offer forgiveness and restoration, the unfortunate truth is that good leaders have been rejected after confessing personal struggles.

Family. One final reason that pastors and leaders do not seek for help is family. Leaders need the comfort of confidentially when resolving hidden issues. Because of their positions, leaders are concerned about their problems being revealed publicly.

The strain that it could bring upon family relations could be seemingly irreversible. Thus, leaders choose to deal with their issues alone to spare their family from undue embarrassment, shame, or break up.

-Chapter 3-

The Recovery of Manasseh

*And prayed unto him: and he was intreated of him (the Lord), and heard his supplication, and brought him again to Jerusalem into his kingdom. Then **Manasseh** knew that the LORD he was God.* ***(2 Chronicles 33:13 NIV*** *Parenthesis mine)*

In the book of 2 Kings, chapter 33, we read of Manasseh becoming king, and how he led the nation in debauchery and wickedness. God allowed Manasseh to be taken prisoner by his enemies.

However, while imprisoned due to the consequences of his rebellion against God, Manasseh sought recovery through prayer. God head him and restored him to his throne.

> *And prayed unto him: and he was intreated of him (the Lord), and heard his supplication, and brought him again to Jerusalem into his kingdom. Then **Manasseh** knew that the LORD he was God.*
> *(2 Chronicles 33:13 NIV Parenthesis mine)*

Steps for Pastors/Leaders

Manasseh's story reveals that there is recovery even after a fall. God heard Manasseh after he took the first step in seeking after God.

Pastors and leaders today also can take certain steps to recover after a fall.

Pride, embarrassment, security, hopelessness and, and family are the major reasons among many why pastors and leaders continue to minister and counsel without receiving ministry. However, these two questions remain:

1. *"How can leaders find counsel and support for the issues in their lives?"*
2. *"How can pastors make their congregations a place of ministry and restoration for their parishioners?"*

There are certain keys that pastors and leaders must use in order to unlock the door to freedom from issues.

Humility

Leaders have to be willing to admit there is a problem. The scriptures say that confession is made unto salvation (Romans 10:10).

Before Christ is received, sin and guilt before God has to be acknowledged. It is then that one can receive Him. Likewise, leaders have to humble themselves (like Manasseh) and admit the truth about themselves and their situations.

It is unprofitable to rationalize sin and weakness. Humility demands honesty within and to God. God will supply grace to those who are humble.

> But he giveth more grace. Wherefore he saith, God resisteth the proud, but giveth grace unto the humble. (James 4:6)

Overcome Fear

Humility is the beginning. However, admittance without action is useless. Once confession is made, the next step is to overcome fear. Four out of the five reasons for pastors and leaders not receiving help are the offspring of fear.

Whatever fears may be present, leaders must take control. Fears have to be presented at the foot of the cross. Pastors and leaders have to remember that God has not given us the spirit of fear. Fear has to be dispelled.

For God hath not given us the spirit of fear; but of power, and of love, and of a sound mind. (2 Timothy 1:7)

Ask

The Bible says that you have not, because you do not ask (James 4:2b). After humbling themselves and overcoming fears, leaders have to ask for help. Though leaders may have to be selective, it should not deter them from seeking guidance.

There are ministries designed to aid pastors

and leaders. If pastors feel they cannot receive the best help possible from within, then they have to seek help from outside sources.

A little research is needed depending on the need, but help is available. Again, leaders must be willing to admit their problems and ask for help.

Listen/Follow Through

Pastors and leaders understand that information without application is useless. Once counsel is received, leaders have to follow the directives given to them.

> *But be ye doers of the word, and not hearers only, deceiving your own selves. (James 1:22)*

Leaders have to resist a "know it all" mentality. Pastors and leaders are accustomed to dispensing advice, but they have to know how to take it. Proverbs tells us that wise men hear.

Leaders who truly want help will listen and take action.

Accountability

After receiving counsel, pastors and leaders should submit to some form of accountability. It is imperative to have individuals that they can confide in.

In addition, leaders can benefit from persons who challenge them in their walk with God and their ministries. Accountability is a necessary precaution, so that they can maintain a life of purity and integrity.

-Chapter 4-

Creating an Atmosphere

THE BELIEVER'S GUIDE TO THE PASTORL MINISTRY A Comprehensive Study of the Pastoral Ministry in the Church

The pastor must hold to principles of holy living through love.

THE BELIEVER'S GUIDE TO THE PASTORL MINISTRY — A Comprehensive Study of the Pastoral Ministry in the Church

Since pastors have the oversight of numerous people, they have the ability to transform their congregations into places of God's healing and restoration for parishioners who have secret struggles. This can be done in a practical manner.

Messages of Love

First, pastors may preach and teach messages whose central themes are love, deliverance, forgiveness, accountability, and restoration for a prescribed length of time.

The messages should be forthright. The pastor must hold to principles of holy living through love. In this way the believer can be reminded that part of the new birth is the ability to overcome personal sins and weakness.

It does demand discipline, but through the help of the indwelling Spirit, and the support of others, recovery remains a stabilizing influence in the believer's heart and mind.

Motivate the Leaders

Second, pastors may hold private sessions with other leaders in the congregation. The focus on these meetings is to create, first, an atmosphere among the leaders whereby they can feel secure in the love and support of one another. The result should be a system of accountability among the leaders.

Third, pastors should instruct these leaders on how to implement teachings and programs around themes of love, acceptance, forgiveness, and restoration in Christ.

Mobilize the Masses

Bible study, youth groups, and Sunday school class instructors will promote this theme in these settings. In this manner, the whole congregation will be involved in the healing and restoration of one another.

Pastors and leaders are placed in the Body of Christ to help men and women overcome and cope with the struggles of life. Their ministries are less effective when they have unresolved issues.

Clergy and laity have to relieve leaders of undue pressure, so that they can receive ministry. In turn, they will able to fulfill their God-given ministries without hindrances from personal issues.

In addition, pastors should shape their local assemblies into places where individuals are given the opportunity to receive forgiveness and counsel without reproach. The result is a vibrant, healthy church.

THE BELIEVER'S GUIDE TO
THE PASTORL MINISTRY A Comprehensive Study of the Pastoral Ministry in the Church

-Book 4-

The Perfecting of the Pastoral Person:

The Preparation of the Pastoral Person for

Ministry and Service

Introduction

Ministry and service in the kingdom of God is a privilege. God calls every member of the Body of Christ to serve for the benefit and welfare of the Body of Christ. However, we must remember that there are personal preparations that God requires for service.

The Potter's Wheel Study Series is designed to help believers recognize and apply the personal preparation that God implements for those called to minister and to serve.

It is our prayer that the minister and the laymen will respond to God's personal preparations for ministry and service.

THE BELIEVER'S GUIDE TO THE PASTORL MINISTRY   A Comprehensive Study of the Pastoral Ministry in the Church

In this Publication

From the scriptures, we discover that the pastoral ministry was seemingly the last on display in the New Testament Church. Its role in the Church has been influential from its inception. However, not everyone in the Church is a pastor. There is diversity in the Body of Christ.

> *Now ye are the body of Christ, and members in particular. And God hath set some in the church, first apostles, secondarily prophets, thirdly teachers, after that miracle, then gifts of healings, helps, governments, diversities of tongues. Are all apostles? Are all prophets? Are all teachers? Are*

all workers miracles? Have all the gifts of healing? Do all speak with tongues? Do all interpret? (I Corinthians 12:27-31)

Since our body has many parts, so does the Body of Christ. Paul explained that the Church was the same as a physical body. He taught that the Body of Christ was made up of many members and that each had a particular function.

He concluded this portion of his argument by showing how God developed offices and gifts in the Church beginning with the apostles.

Afterwards, to illustrate further his point of diversity, he asks a series of questions to which the answer is a resounding "NO!" All are not apostles and all are not prophets, and so on.

Since all are not pastors, God makes the benefit of pastoral ministry available to all by placing a pastoral anointing on other members in the Body.

In this book, we will examine those who possess a pastoral grace and endowment. Those possessing a pastoral anointing are referred to as pastoral people. They have a passion for Christ and the Church. In addition, we will consider how God perfects the pastoral person for service in the Church.

The pastoral anointing is as broad as the pastoral office. However, there are certain characteristics that pastoral individuals share. No matter what their individual functions are in the Church, pastoral people will exhibit the characteristics of undershepherds and men/maidservants.

THE BELIEVER'S GUIDE TO
THE PASTORL MINISTRY

A Comprehensive Study of the Pastoral Ministry in the Church

-Prologue-
Understanding Anointings

Today, believers worldwide have developed an appreciation for spiritual gifts and manifestations. However, misinterpretations of scripture have caused individuals to boast in possessing "anointings" that do not exist.

Before exploring the teaching anointing, we must develop a clear understanding of the anointing.

Both the Old and New Testaments contain numerous references to the anointing. The anointing is an important component in the service of the Lord. Under both covenants, the servants of the Lord could not serve without it.

The Hebrew and Greek terms for "to

anoint" denote to smear or rub in. This implies that the anointing becomes a part of the individual who has received it.

Anointings in the Old Testament

The scriptures tell us that there are diversities of anointings. This was true even under the Old Covenant.

The Hebrew term for anointing was mashchah (pronounced mash-khaw'). It means a consecratory gift and also to consecrate. This implies that the anointed individuals were gifts to those they ministered to.

In addition, they were set aside unto

the purpose for which they were anointed.

In the Old Testaments texts, God anointed individuals to perform various tasks and stand in certain offices. They were anointed to stand in the offices of priest and king, through oil being poured upon them.

Aaron anointed as a priest

> *And thou shalt put them upon Aaron thy brother, and his sons with him; and shalt anoint them, and consecrate them, and sanctify them, that they may minister unto me in the priest's office. (Exodus 28: 41)*

David anointed king by Samuel

> *Then Samuel took the horn of oil, and*

> *and anointed him in the midst of his brethren: and the Spirit of the Lord came upon David (I Samuel 16: 13a)*

In each of these examples, the anointing of God was demonstrated by a physical anointing of the individual. However, others were anointed to stand in positions of authority without an outward anointing.

The Judges

> *Nevertheless the Lord raised up judges, which delivered them out of the hand of those that spoiled them. (Judges 2:16)*

The Prophets

> *Since the day that your fathers came forth out of the land of Egypt unto this day I have even sent unto you all my servants the prophets, daily rising up early and sending them. (Jeremiah 7:25)*

It is clear that God raised up the judges and prophets to stand in positions of great authority without an anointing ceremony. The Spirit of God anointed them. We discover that no one could function in any of the above offices except God placed them.

Though there were other individuals whom the Lord used, we find that God anointed individuals to stand as prophets, judges, priests, and kings continually.

In addition, there were other individuals anointed by God to function in other capacities without an anointing ceremony.

Individuals such as the builders of the tabernacle, the seventy elders who prophesied after receiving Moses' spirit, Barak, Ezra, Nehemiah, Zerubbabel, and various others. They received an anointing from God to accomplish specific tasks.

Anointings in the New Testament

After Christ's resurrection and the outpouring of the Spirit, we find that God still anointed individuals for service. We discover from the scriptures that men and women are anointed to stand in ministry offices such as apostles, prophets, evangelists, pastors, and teachers.

> *And he gave some, apostles; and some, prophets; and some, evangelists; and some, pastors and teachers. (Ephesians 4:11)*

Likewise, aside from functioning in ministry offices, individuals are anointed and endowed with certain gifts for Christian service. These other gifts and offices are listed in the book of I Corinthians and in the Book of Romans.

> *But the manifestation of the Spirit is*

to one is given by the Spirit the word of wisdom; to another the word of knowledge by the same Spirit; To another faith by the same Spirit; to another the gifts of healing by the same Spirit; To another the working of miracles; to another prophecy; to another discerning of spirits; to another divers kinds of tongues; to another the interpretation of tongues. (I Corinthians 12:7-10)

Having then gifts differing according to the grace that is given to us, whether prophecy, let us prophesy according to the proportion of faith; Or ministry, let us wait on our ministering: or he that

> *teacheth, on teaching; Or he that exhorteth, on exhortation: he that giveth, let him do it with simplicity; he that ruleth, with diligence; he that sheweth mercy, with cheerfulness. (Romans 12:6-8)*

Though various terms are used in the New Testament to describe the anointing of the Spirit, two terms are seen frequently. The first is found in II Corinthians 2:21,

> *Now he which stablisheth us with you in Christ, and hath anointed us, is God. (2 Corinthians 1:21 KJV)*

The Greek work for anointed in this text is chrio (pronounced khree'-o). It means to be consecrated to an office or religious service. Paul used this term to express that God had placed him in the apostolic office to minister to the Church.

Thus, we find that one receives an anointing to serve. If you are not called to a ministry office, there is an anointing on you to serve in some capacity. The second term used for anointing is found in I John 2:20,

> *But the anointing which ye have received of him abideth in you, and ye need not that any man teach you: but as the same anointing teacheth you of all things, and is truth, and is no lie, and even as it hath taught you, ye shall abide in him. (I John 2:27 KJV)*

The Greek word used here is chrisma (pronounced khris'-mah). We derive the word charisma from this word. It is defined as the special endowment of the Holy Spirit. Hence, the anointing comes with gifts and endowments from God.

Therefore, as believers, we should consider the use of the expression, "I am anointed to do such and such" carefully. We must not confuse personal gifts and talents with the endowment of the Spirit.

When we receive the Spirit of God, its presence abides in us. The same is true for the anointing. When God places a particular anointing upon an individual, it remains. The gifts of God will operate according to the need and purpose of the moment.

However, the "anointings" or endowments of the Spirit abide with an individual at all times. Even in disobedience, the anointing to be king remained upon Saul. David recognized this (I Samuel 24:6).

Office versus Anointing

The Spirit of God governs all of the spiritual activities within the Body. He anoints and appoints according to the ultimate will of the Father.

Since the Body of Christ is made up of many members, there are various needs within it. The Spirit of God then anoints individuals to fulfill the needs within the Body.

The greatest burden for ministry rests upon the leaders, specifically, the apostles, prophets, evangelists, pastors, and teachers. Their purpose is found in Ephesians 4:12:

1. 1.To perfect the saints

2. To train them for the work of the ministry

3. To build up the Church spiritually

However, these ministries are not responsible to minister to everyone. God uses the entire Body of Christ. The members of the Body of Christ are called to minister to one another, even if they are not called to a ministry office.

> *As every man hath received the gift, even so minister the same one toward another, as good stewards over the manifold grace of God. (I Peter 4:10)*

Therefore, God anoints individuals to function in similar ways to those of the ministry offices.

Believers will have anointings on their lives, which, if not careful, may be mistaken for a call to a particular ministry office. This implies that there are some that have an apostolic gift without being called as an apostle.

Moreover, some have an anointing to prophesy without functioning in the office of the prophet. This is also true for teachers.

Numerous individuals today have laid claim to a pastoral anointing without understanding all that they entail. Remember to never confuse a call to a ministry office with an anointing of the Holy Spirit. However, an individual with a pastoral anointing is identified as a pastoral person.

With this brief analysis of the anointing, we will now explore the pastoral anointing and how God prepares one for this gift and ministry in the Church.

-Chapter 1-

Pastoral People are Undershepherds

THE BELIEVER'S GUIDE TO THE PASTORL MINISTRY | A Comprehensive Study of the Pastoral Ministry in the Church

Pastoral people are endowed with shepherding gifts that will reflect the love of the Good Shepherd while they serve with the local pastor of the Church. They will fulfill pastoral functions under the direction of established leadership. They will fully support the pastor in his ministry to the Church.

Spiritual Providers

Undershepherds provide for the sheep. Pastoral people will look out for their brothers and sisters in Christ.

They will endeavor to make sure they have the necessary tools and support to make it in their walks with the Lord.

The Lord is my shepherd; I shall not

want. (Psalm 23:1)

Pastoral people will endeavor to help others receive what they need to live a victorious Christian life. God set pastoral people in the Church to reveal the love and comfort of the Good Shepherd.

Spiritual Imparters

Undershepherds feed the flock with wisdom and knowledge. A natural shepherd leads the flock to places where they can be nourished with food and water.

The undershepherd helps the shepherd in the care of the flock. Pastoral people will provide sound biblical insight to promote growth and stability in the Church.

He maketh me to lie down in green pastures: he leadeth me beside the still waters. (Psalm 23:2)

Spiritual Discipline

Undershepherds correct and comfort the sheep of the fold. A natural shepherd carries a rod and staff. The staff is designed to keep the flock together, while the rod is designed to bring a sheep back into the fold when it runs away.

...thy rod and thy staff they comfort me. (Psalm 23:4b)

Pastoral individuals will not be afraid to challenge others in their walks with the Lord. They will not be afraid to reveal hindrances in the lives of others. They not only will challenge others, but also help them to overcome in any known areas of fault or weakness.

> *Brethren, if a man be overtaken in a fault, ye which are spiritual, restore such an one in the spirit of meekness; considering thyself, lest thou also be tempted. Bear ye one another's burdens, and so fulfill the law of Christ. (Galatians 6:1-2)*

Spiritual Protectors

Undershepherds protect the flock. A natural shepherd protects the sheep against wolves and thieves. He is willing to put in his life in jeopardy for the lives of the sheep.

I am the good shepherd: the good shepherd giveth his life for the sheep. (John 10:11)

Pastoral people will help others to follow established godly leadership and to avoid false ministers and doctrines.

They will protect other saints by looking out for their benefit. They know how to bear the infirmities of others to provide protection against spiritual deception.

-Chapter 2-

Pastoral People are Menservansts & Maidservants

THE BELIEVER'S GUIDE TO THE PASTORL MINISTRY — A Comprehensive Study of the Pastoral Ministry in the Church

Pastoral people believe that greatness in the kingdom of God begins with selfless service in the Church. Servants obey their masters. Pastoral people will be true servants in the Church. They not only will obey Christ but established godly leadership.

They will endeavor to see the Church advance and the members as well. Not only will they be subject to leadership, but more importantly to the Word of God and the leading of His Spirit.

A Servant's Care

Servants care for their master's children. Pastoral people will have a love for the people of God.

Even as a natural servant sometimes is responsible for the master's children, pastoral people believe that they are their brother's keeper and will seek for their continual salvation in the Church.

Brethren, if any of you do err from the truth, and one convert him; Let him know, that he which converteth the sinner from the error of his way shall save a soul from death, and shall hide a multitude of sins. (James 5:19-20)

A Servant's Submission

Servants keep their master's ordinance even in their absence. Pastoral people will never abuse any authority given to them by leadership or God. They will strive for the unity of the Church.

They will promote godly leadership and follow leadership wholeheartedly. They will support the pastor as he follows the leading of Christ in the Church.

THE BELIEVER'S GUIDE TO THE PASTORL MINISTRY — A Comprehensive Study of the Pastoral Ministry in the Church

-Chapter 3-

Character Traits of Pastoral People

Because pastoral people have unique gifts, they must strive to reflect the nature of Christ at all times and resist pride. Paul gives the necessary character traits of pastoral people in his instructions to the Roman Church (Romans 12:9-17).

These traits are the prescribed for those who possess a pastoral anointing.

Love of the Body of Christ

Pastoral people have to demonstrate genuine love. They must be lovers of good and despisers of evil in all forms. (Romans 12:9)

Pastoral people must love the brethren and seek the welfare of others above themselves. (Romans 12:10)

Faithful in the Body of Christ

Pastoral people have to resist procrastination and stagnation in ministry. They must maintain a zeal for the work of the Lord. (Romans 12:11)

Pastoral people have to be people of faith and prayer. They have to be able to endure tribulation, inspire hope in others and themselves, and be prayer warriors. (Romans 12:12)

Pastoral people have to be selfless. They must be willing to meet the needs of others and to be easily entreated. (Romans 12:13)

Building of the Body of Christ

Pastoral people should speak words that edify and build up other believers at all times. They are not to be gossips and revilers. (Romans 12:14)

Pastoral people have to be in tune with other members of the Body. They, through the Spirit, have to be sensitive to the failures, trials, and successes of others. (Romans 12:15)

Pastoral people have to be impartial in their relationships with others. They should be as God who is no respecter of persons. (Romans 12:16)

Pastoral people have to be harmless.

They ought to be gentle, representing the nature of God in all honesty. (Romans 12:17)

Anyone who feels he/she has a pastoral anointing has to guard themselves against pride, deception, and visions of greatness. In turn, they will be pillars in the midst of the Church.

-Chapter 4-

Realizing the Pastoral Anointing

THE BELIEVER'S GUIDE TO THE PASTORL MINISTRY — A Comprehensive Study of the Pastoral Ministry in the Church

Pastoral people will function uniquely in the Body of Christ. In order to recognize the pastoral anointing, one must first know what are the functions of pastoral individuals.

Understanding Scriptures

Pastoral people understand the Word of God. Pastoral people understand and know how to make proper application of the scriptures. They, like pastors, will understand many of the foundational truths of God through scripture. They encourage other believers to study the Word of God.

Study to shew thyself approved unto God, a workman that needeth not to be ashamed, rightly dividing the word of

> truth. But shun profane and vain babblings: for they will increase unto more ungodliness. (II Timothy 2:15)

Understanding Impartation

Pastoral people impart life into other believers. Pastoral people know how to communicate spiritual truths to help other believers grow in the knowledge of the Lord. Their words will consistently minister grace, wisdom, insight, hope, and faith to those around them.

> Let no corrupt communication proceed out of your mouth, but that which is good to the use of edifying, that it may minister grace unto the hearers. (Ephesians 4:29)

Pastoral people help establish others in their walks with the Lord. Pastoral people have the spiritual insight to help babes and immature saints gain strength in the Lord. Like pastors, they will help them to overcome weaknesses and sins through wise counsel, prayer, and support.

> *Brethren, if a man be overtaken in a fault, ye which are spiritual, restore such an one in the spirit of meekness; considering thyself, lest thou also be tempted. Bear ye one another's burdens, and so fulfill the law of Christ. (Galatians 6:1-2)*

Understanding Prayer

Pastoral people are effective

intercessors. Like pastors, they will spend considerable time in prayer for the Church, leadership, and the other saints. They desire to see the Church and other members of the Body of Christ prosper spiritually and naturally.

> *Praying always with all prayer and supplication in the Spirit, and watching thereunto with all perseverance and supplication for all saints. (Ephesians 6:18)*

Understanding Authority

Pastoral people serve and support leadership. Pastoral people believe in servant hood. They will support godly leadership without question.

No matter what capacity they serve in the Church, it is done as unto the Lord and with respect unto God-given leadership. They also encourage others to follow the leadership as they follow the Lord.

> *Remember them which have the rule over you, who have spoken unto you the word of God: whose faith follow, considering the end of their conversation. (Hebrews 13:17)*

Pastoral people expose false doctrines and ministers. Pastoral people exercise mature discernment. They are zealous for the Lord and the purity of the Church. They have the wisdom to recognize false ministers and doctrines readily. They are bold in identifying the false while supporting the truth.

> *Beware of false prophets, which come to you in sheep's clothing, but inwardly they are ravening wolves. Ye shall know them by their fruits. Do men gather grapes of thorns, or figs of thistles? (Matthew 7:15-16)*

Understanding Gifts

Pastoral people possess the power and gifts of the Spirit. Pastoral people have the gifts in operation in their lives (especially showing of mercy and giving). This enhances their service to others in the assembly. They are believers who have powerful testimonies of the power of God being displayed in their everyday lives.

And these signs shall follow them that believe; In my name shall they cast out devils; they shall speak with new tongues; They shall take up serpents; and if they drink any deadly thing, it shall not hurt them; they shall lay hands on the sick, and they shall recover. (Mark 16:17-18)

Though pastoral people are scattered throughout the Body of Christ, no matter where they are they bring life and stability among the congregation.

-Chapter 5-

Flowing in the Pastoral Anointing

If you believe there is a pastoral anointing upon your life, there are certain practical steps to take to flow properly in it. Without these disciplines in your life, you will never flow fully in what God has for you.

Consistent in Study

Study the Word of God. Pastoral people have to consistently study and apply the Word of God to their lives. The Word has to rule their hearts and minds. The Word will equip them for service in the Body of Christ.

Pastoral people have to believe the scriptures are trustworthy. They must have faith that the Word is directly from God.

All scripture is given by inspiration of God, and is profitable for doctrine, for reproof, for correction, for instruction in righteousness: That the man of God may be perfect, thoroughly furnished unto all good works. (II Timothy 3:16-17)

Consistent in Prayer

Have an established prayer life. Pastoral people have to be consistent in prayer. It is the only way to remain strong in the Lord. In addition, prayer will give them greater sensitivity in the Spirit. Prayer will guide them to their rightful places in ministry. They should have a heart to pray also for local leadership that nothing hinders the spreading of the gospel.

> *Praying always with all prayer and supplication in the Spirit, and watching thereunto with all perseverance and supplication for all saints. (Ephesians 6:18)*

Consistent in Submission

Pastoral people will follow Leadership. Pastoral people have to be submitted to local leadership. They must follow the vision of the leaders as they follow Christ. Without being submitted to authority, they will become ineffective in the Church.

> *Remember them which have the rule over you, who have spoken unto you*

the word of God: whose faith follow, considering the end of their conversation. (Hebrews 13:7)

23 Bibliography

Evans, Roderick L. I Will Give You Pastors: Examining the Pastoral Office in the New Testament Church. Abundant Truth Publishing. Camden, NC, 2009

Lockman Foundation. *Comparative Study Bible.* Zondervan Publishing House. Grand Rapids, MI, c1984

Merriam-Webster Online Dictionary Copyright © 2005 by Merriam-Webster, Incorporated. All rights reserved.

The Bible Library. *The Bible Library CD Rom Disc.* Ellis Enterprises Incorporated, (c) 1988 – 2000. 4205 McAuley Blvd., Suite 385, Oklahoma City, OK 73120. All Rights Reserved.

www.ingramcontent.com/pod-product-compliance
Lightning Source LLC
Chambersburg PA
CBHW050338010526
44119CB00049B/599